# how to draw
## cool things

3dtotal
KIDS

**Email:** publishing@3dtotal.com
**Website:** www.3dtotal.com

First published in the United Kingdom, 2023, by 3dtotal Kids, an imprint of 3dtotal Publishing.

Address: 3dtotal.com Ltd, 29 Foregate Street, Worcester, WR1 1DS, United Kingdom.

Soft cover ISBN: 978-1-912843-75-6
Printed and bound in China
by C&C Offset Printing Co., Ltd

Written & illustrated by Erin Hunting

Editor: Marisa Lewis
Designer: Fiona Tarbet
Lead Editor: Samantha Rigby
Lead Designer: Joseph Cartwright
Studio Manager: Simon Morse
Managing Director: Tom Greenway

At 3dtotal Publishing we give 50% of our net profits to charities that help people, animals, and our planet. We also plant one tree for every book we sell.

Erin Hunting is a Melbourne-based illustrator and character designer who loves to create drawings for picture books and comics.

erinhunting.com

# This book belongs to...

All you'll need is something to draw with:

crayons

pens

pencils

markers

Whatever you like!

And also paper!
It can be loose or in a sketchbook:

So come on, let's have some fun!

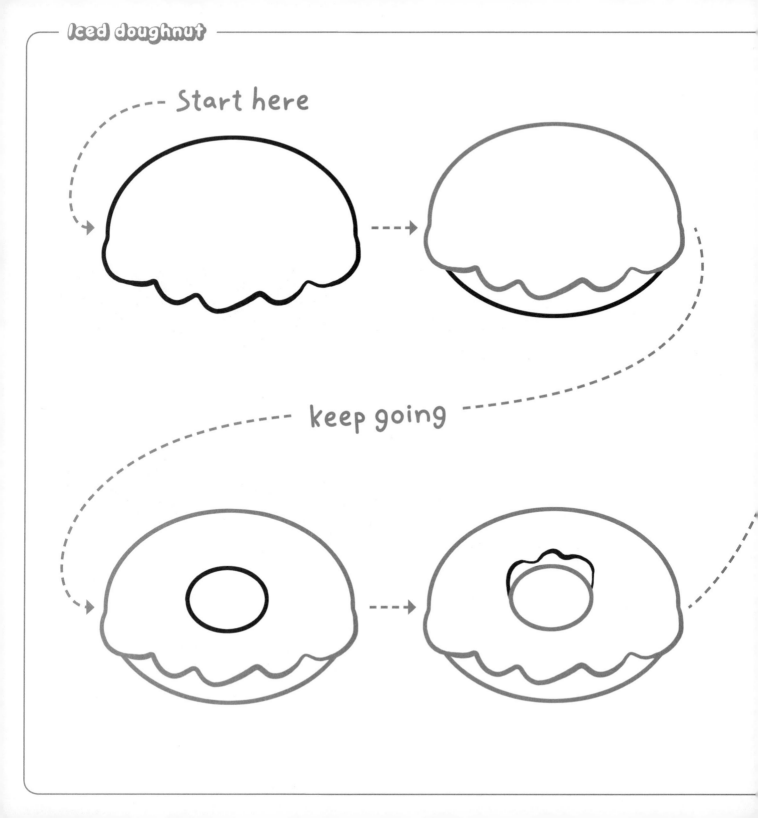

Iced doughnut

Start here

keep going

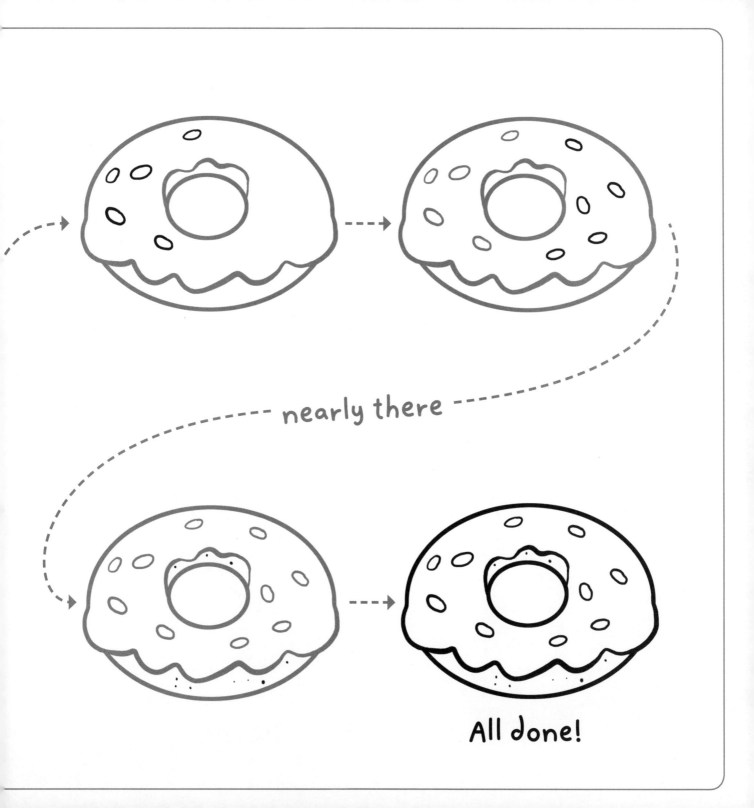

nearly there

All done!

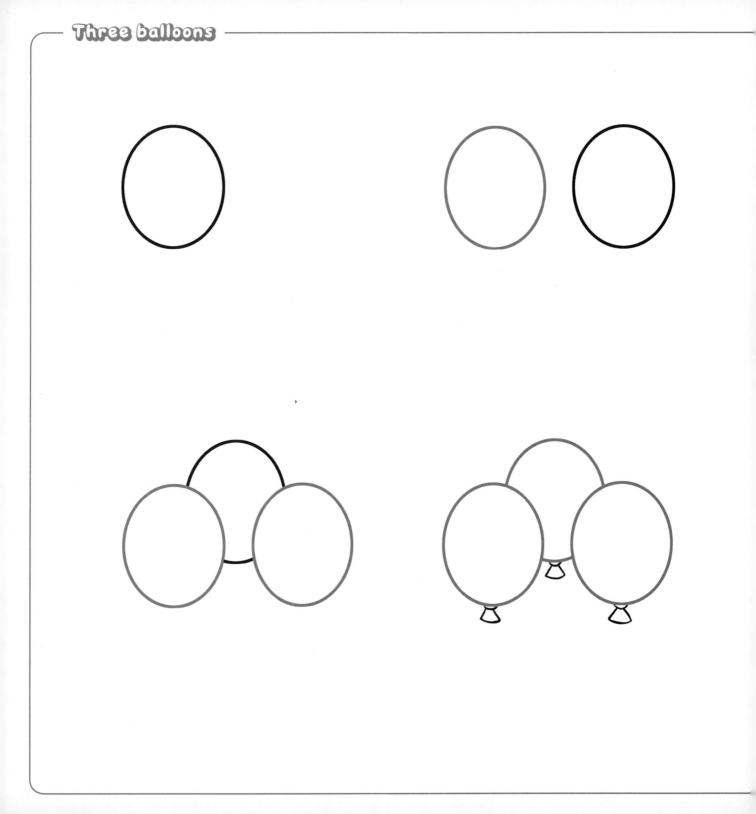

## Big umbrella

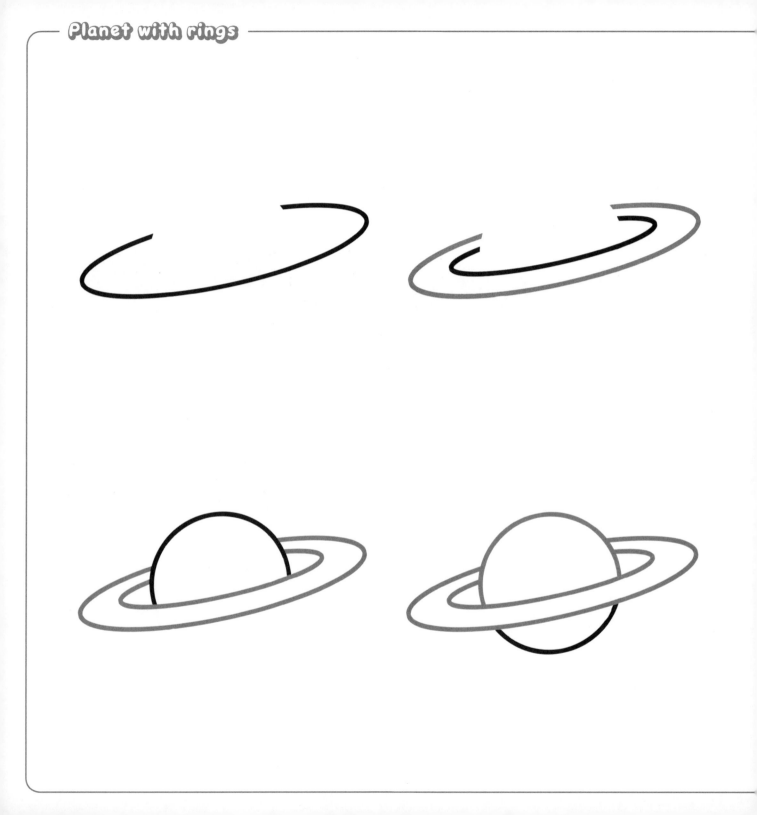

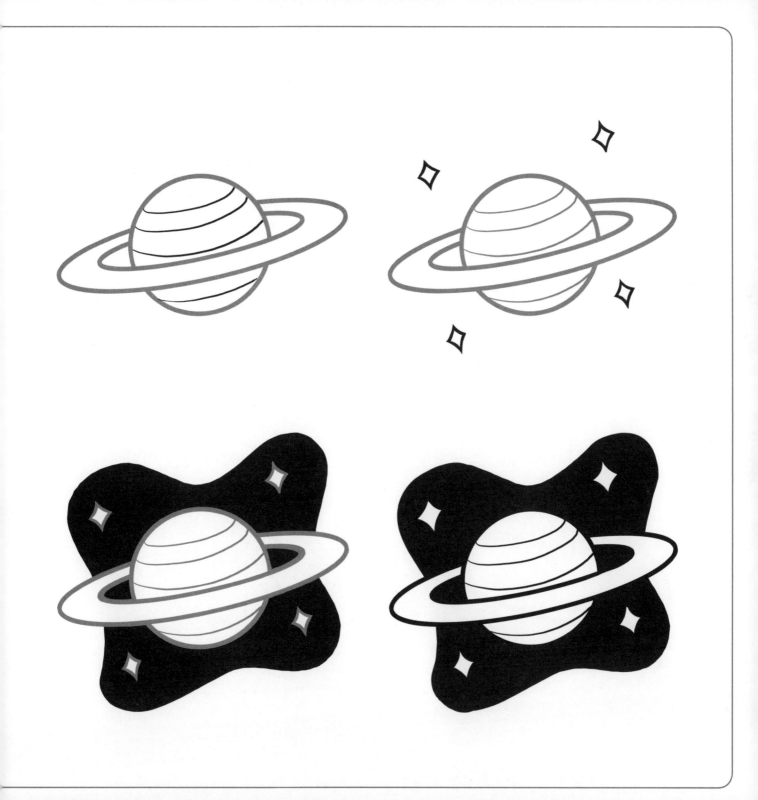

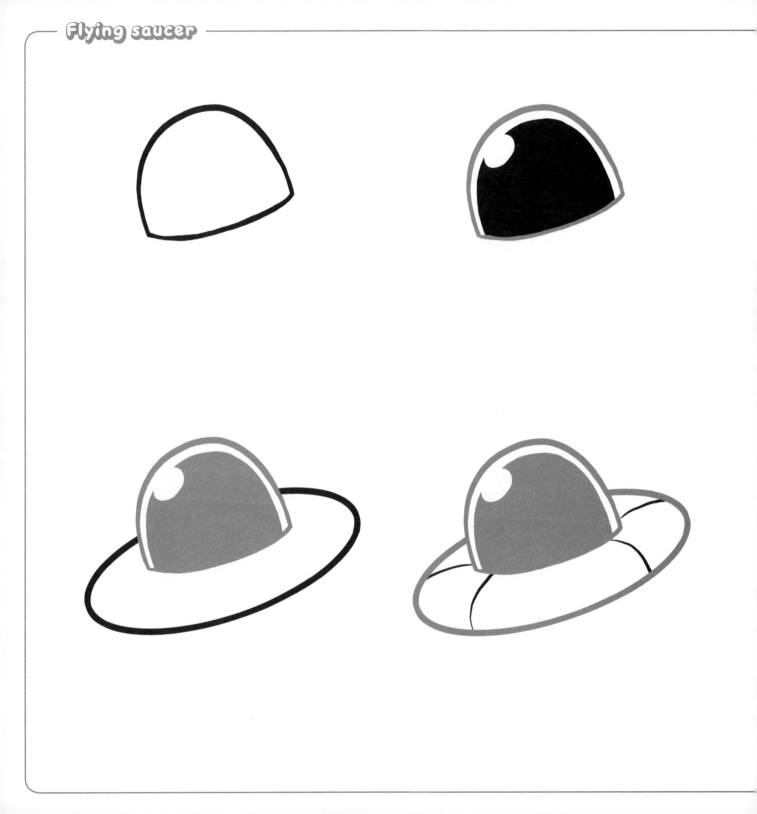

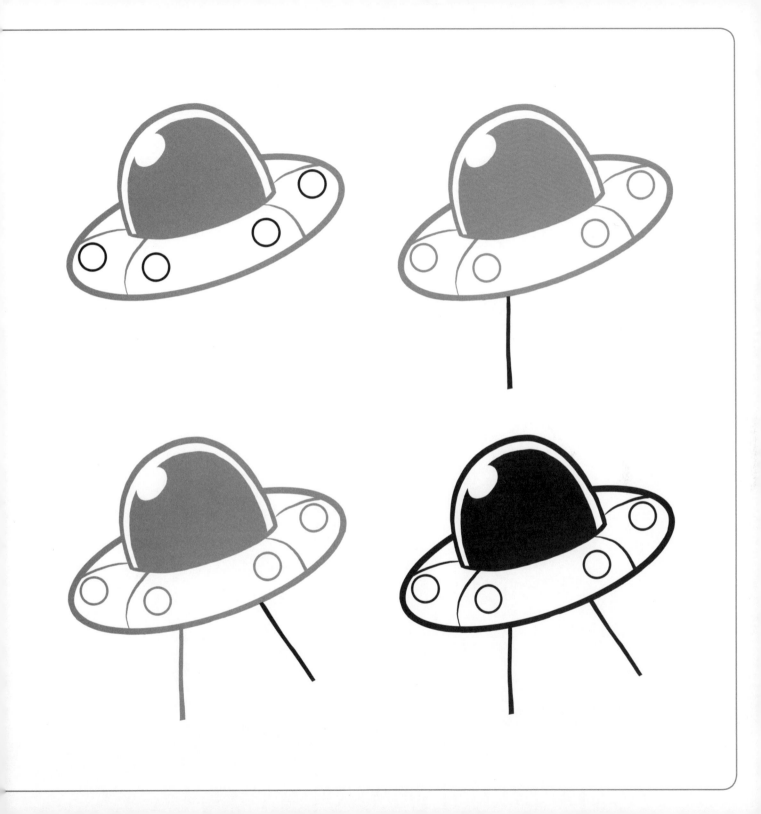

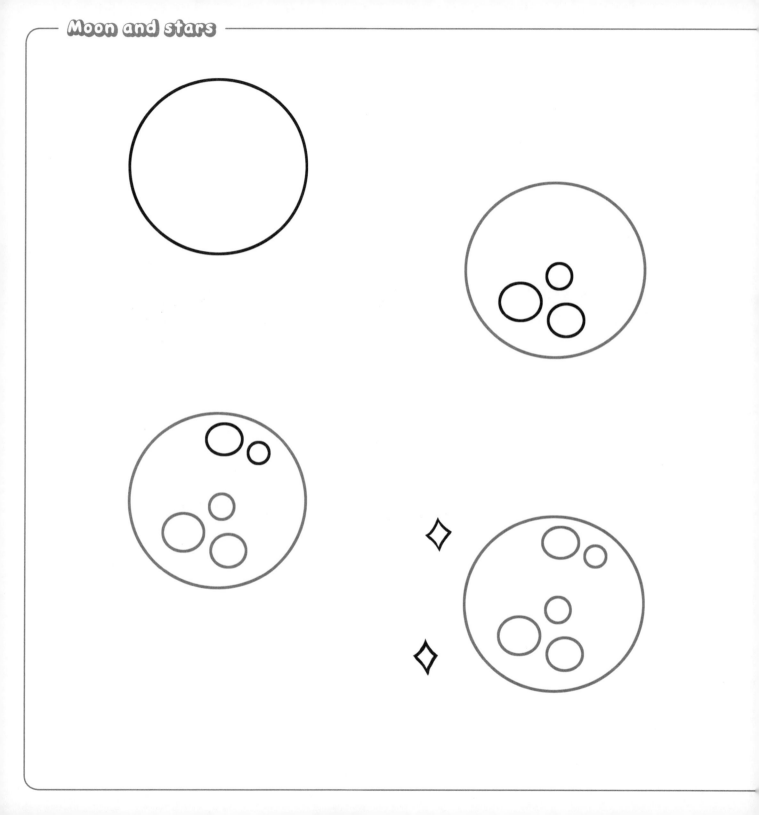

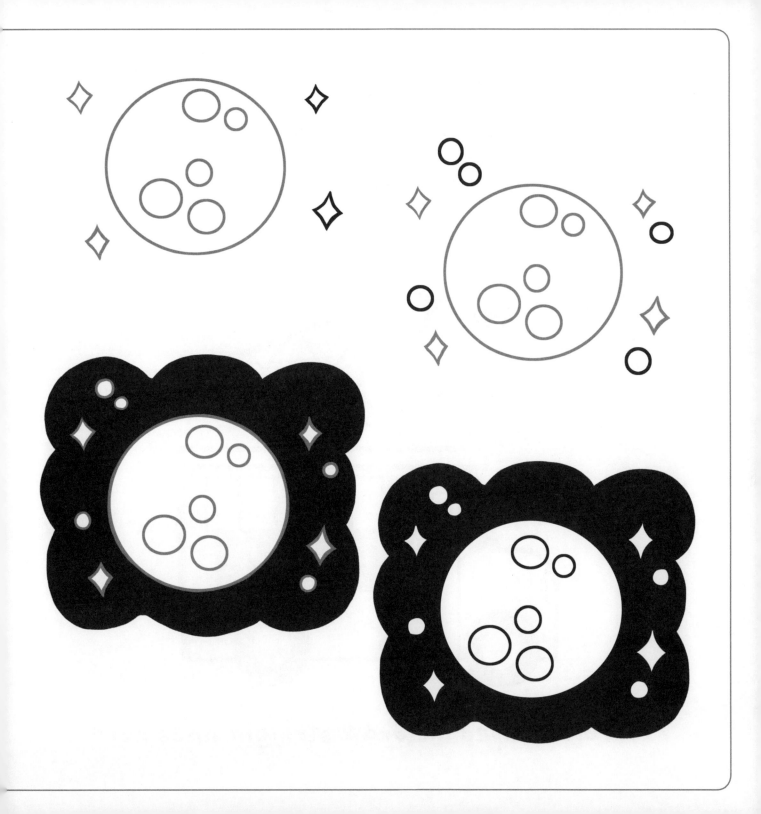

For some drawings with straight lines, you may want to use a ruler.

A ruler helped me draw straight lines here...

...and here, too!

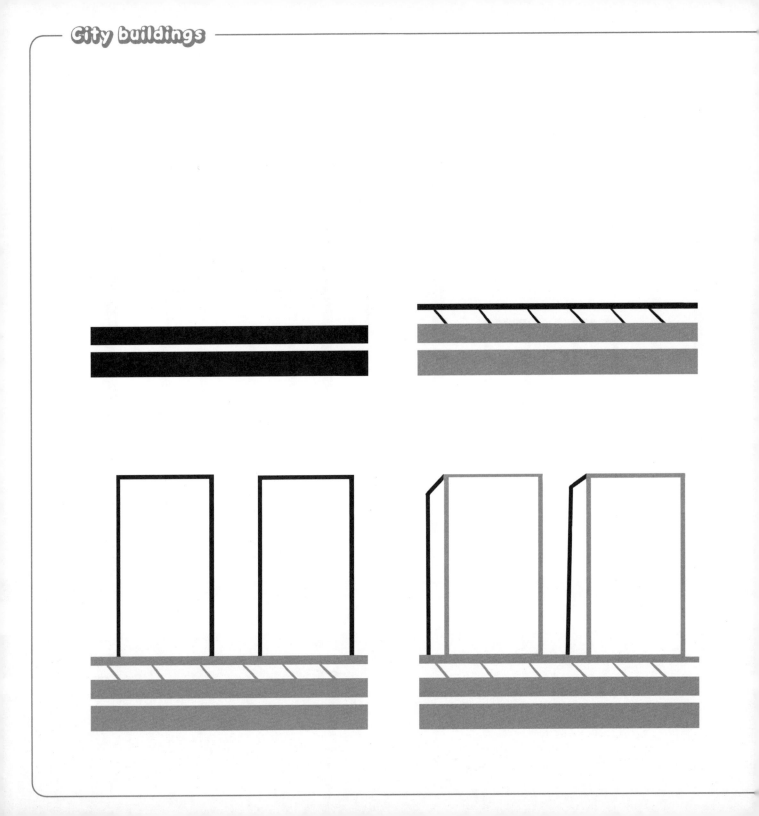

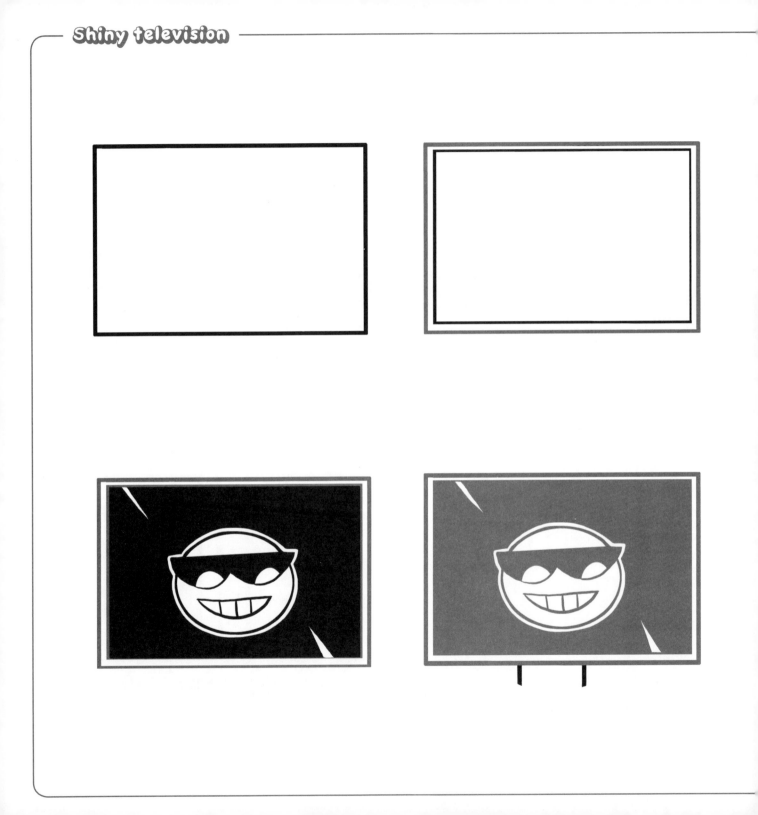

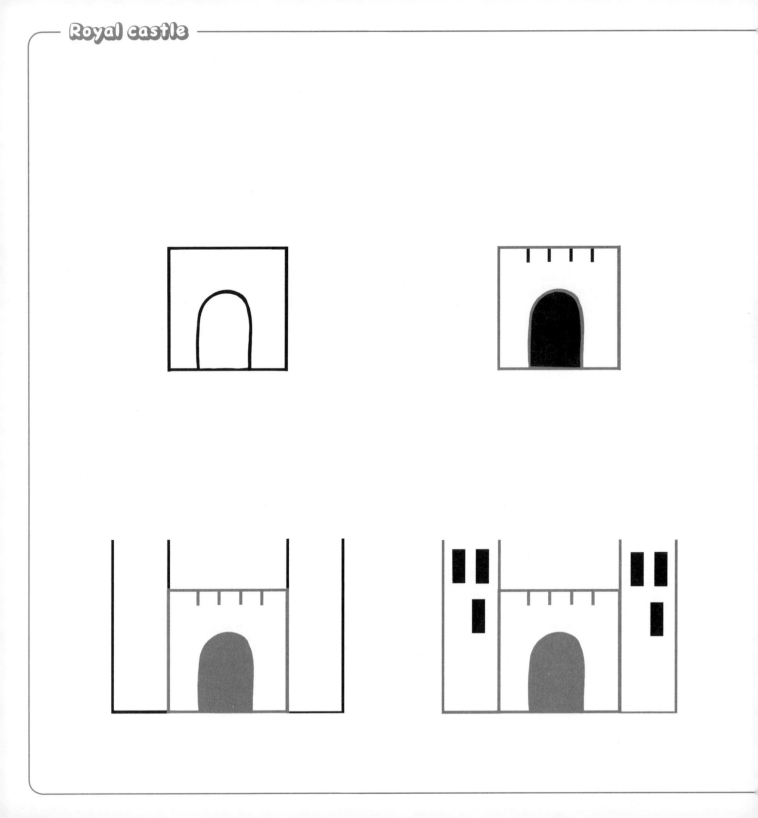

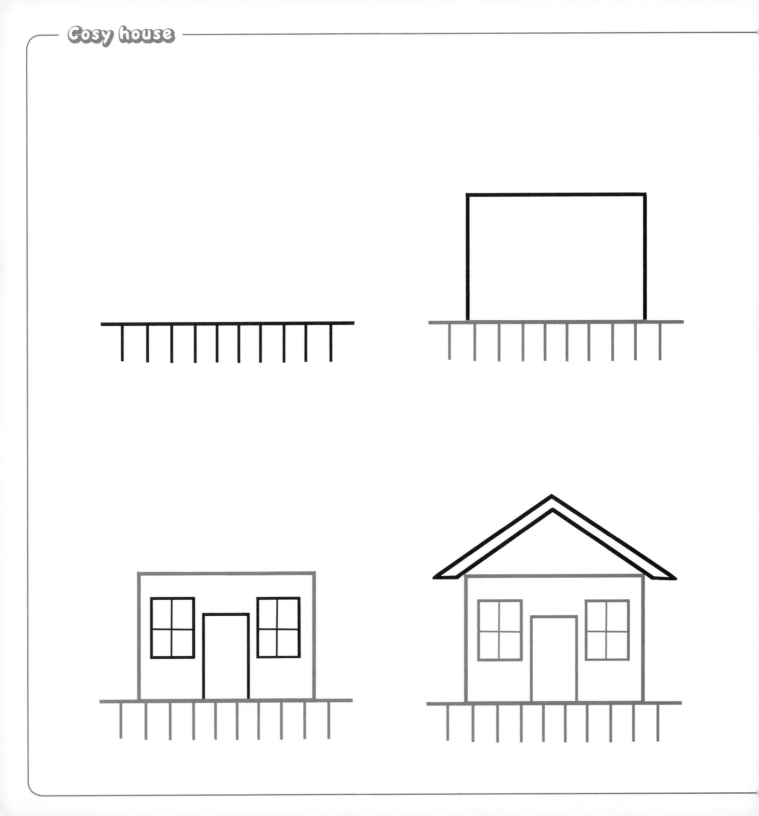

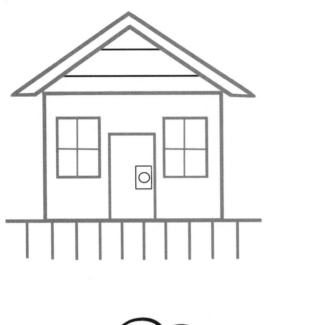

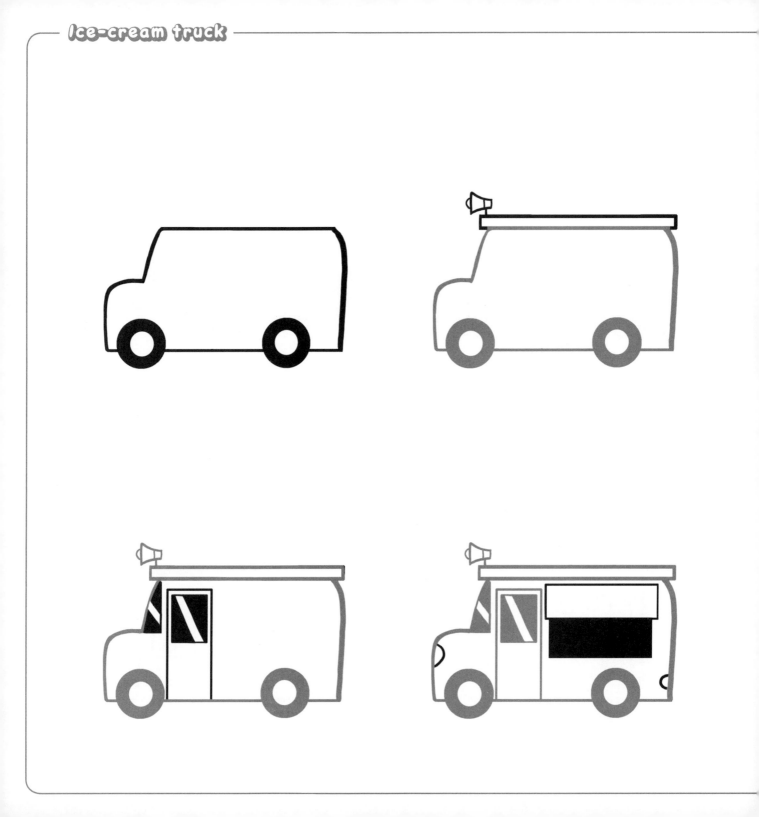

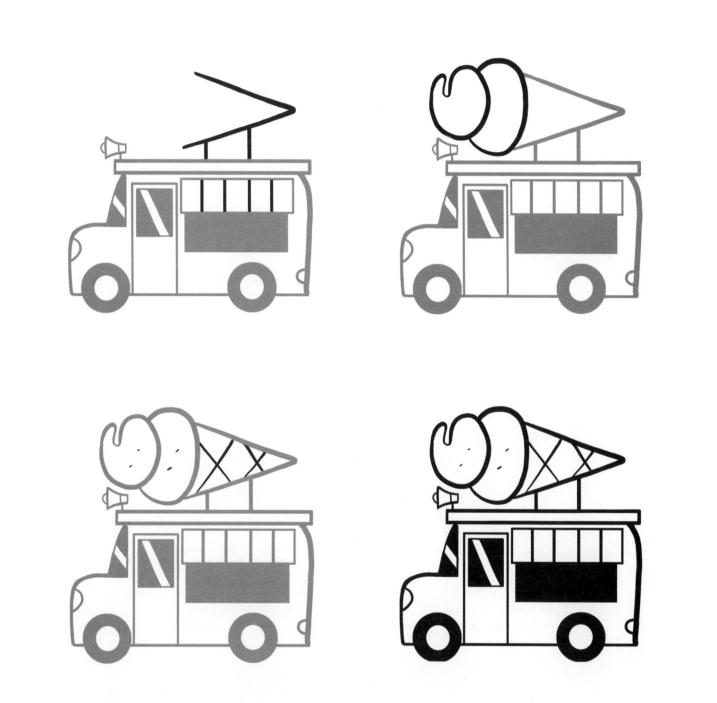

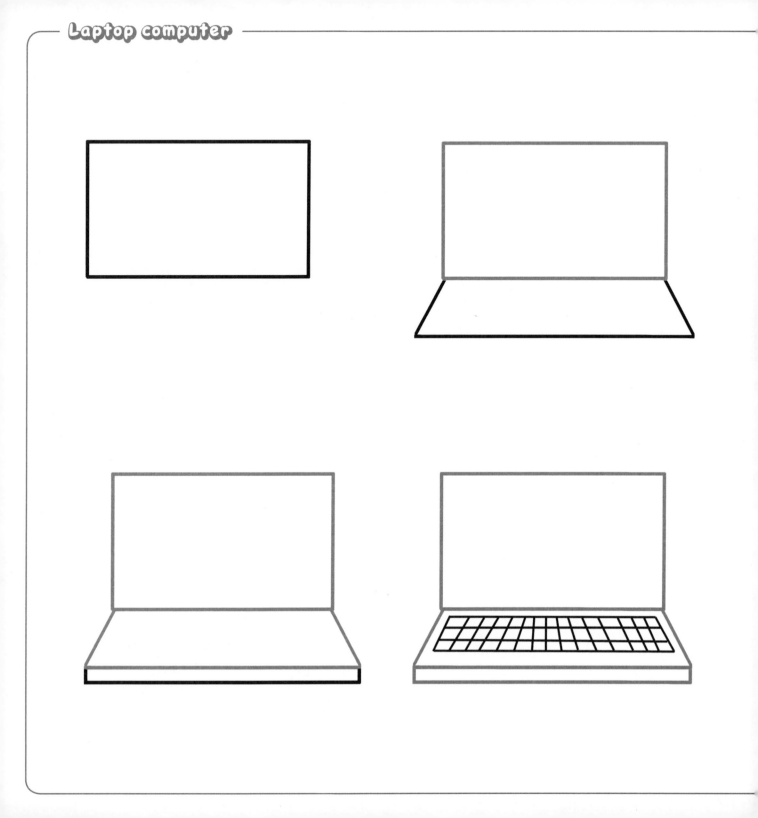

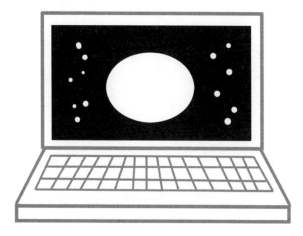
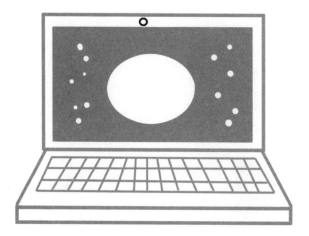

# It's also OK <u>not to use a ruler.</u>
## Freehand lines can work better...

Wavy
underwater lines

Relaxed sailing
lines

Loud stomp lines

Fast straight lines

...especially for drawing objects that are moving!

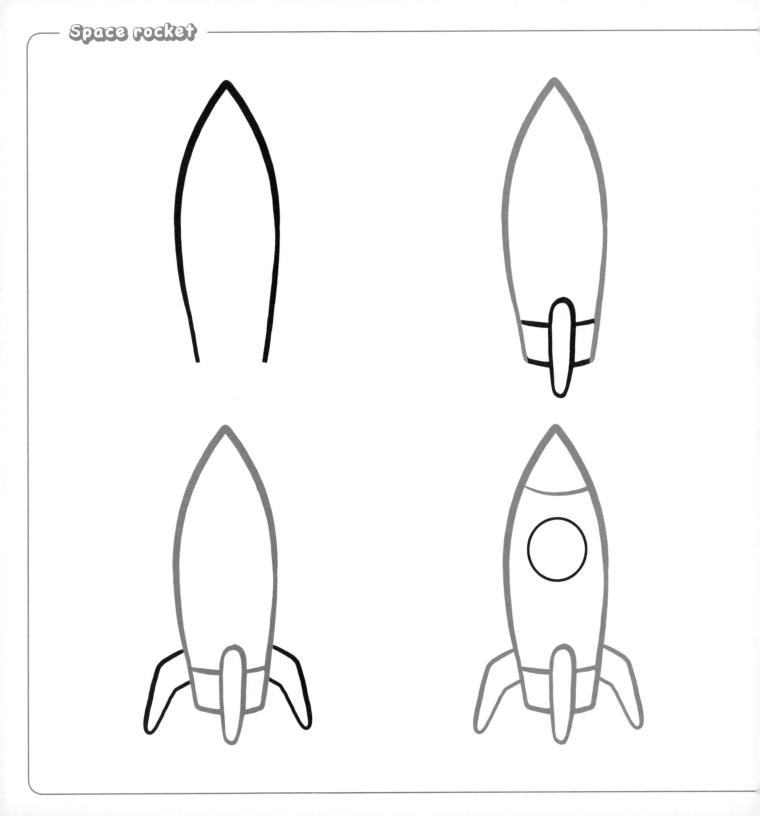

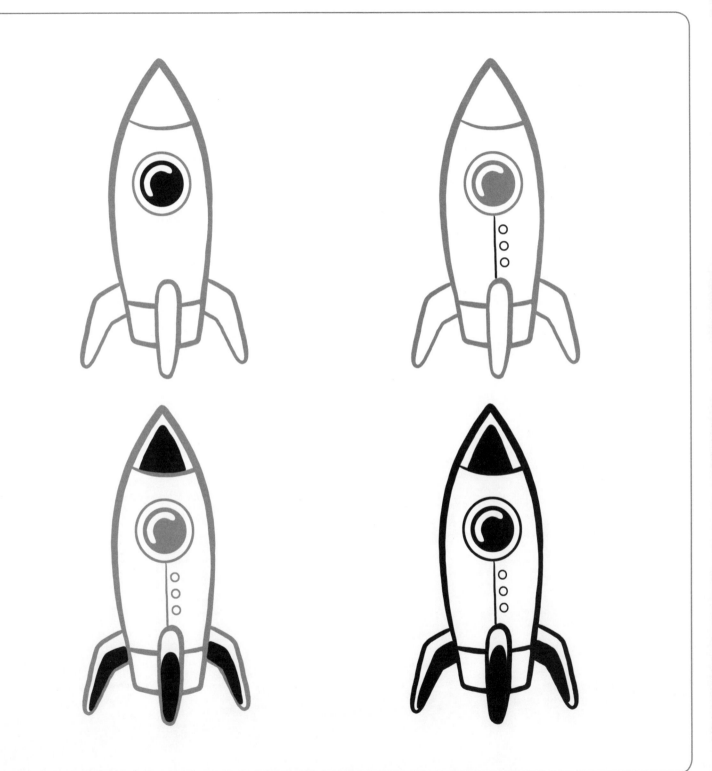

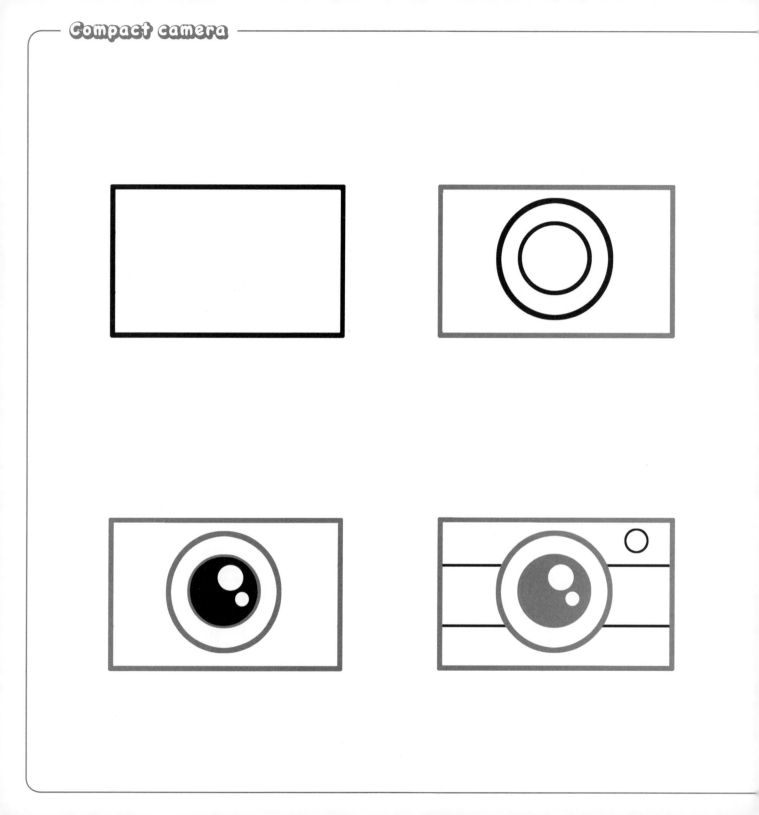

Compact camera

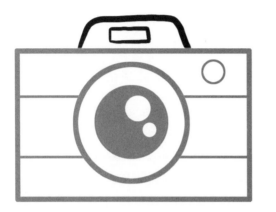 

 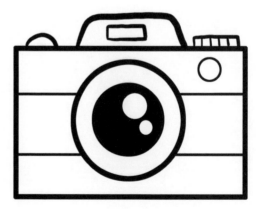

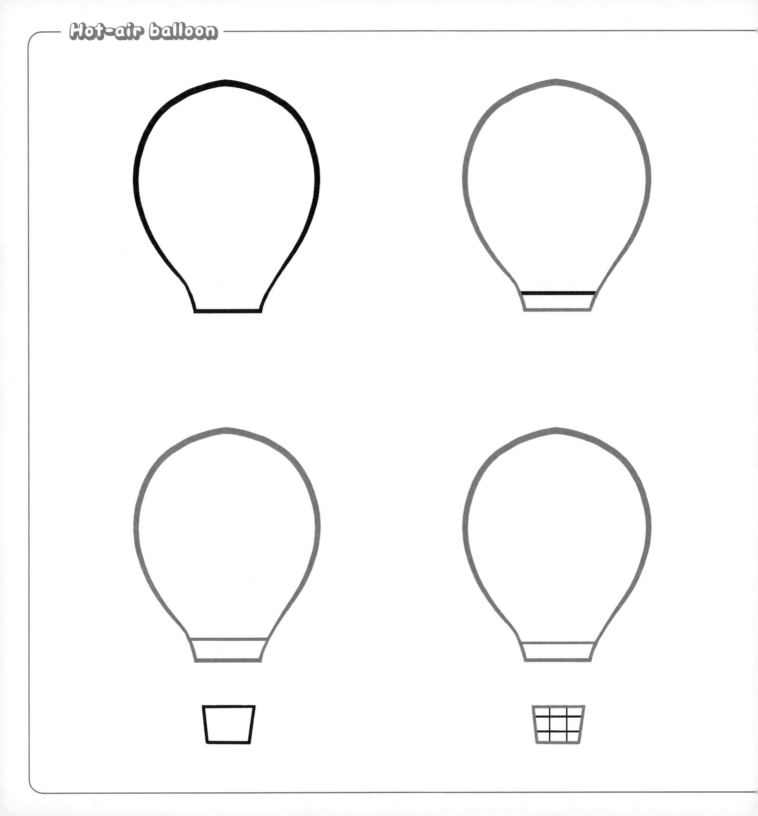

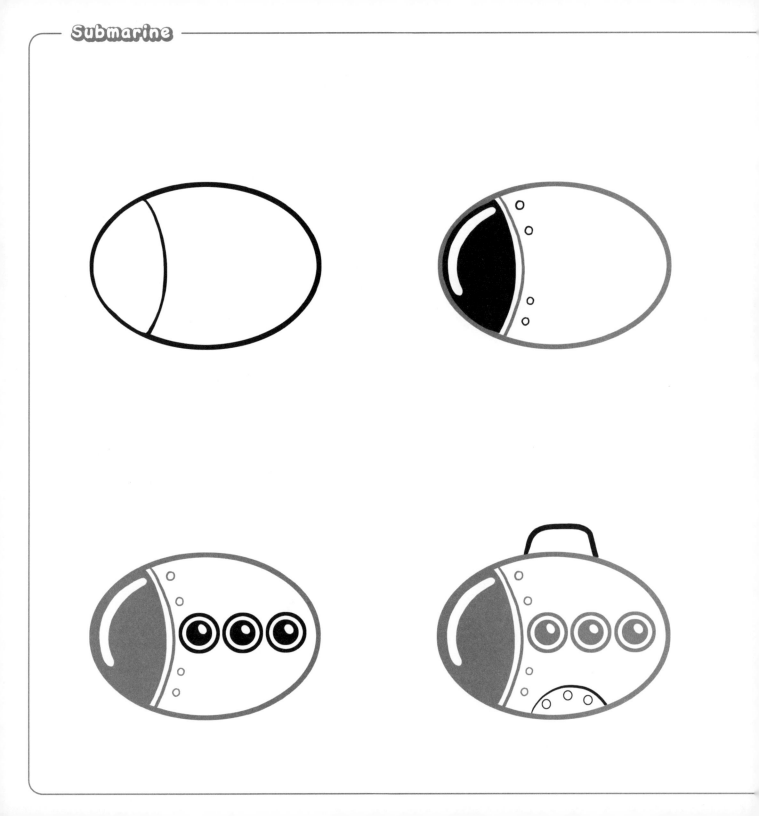

Drawing with **thick** and thin lines can make an object look better and more interesting.

This controller and umbrella would look too crowded if the lines were all too **thick**!

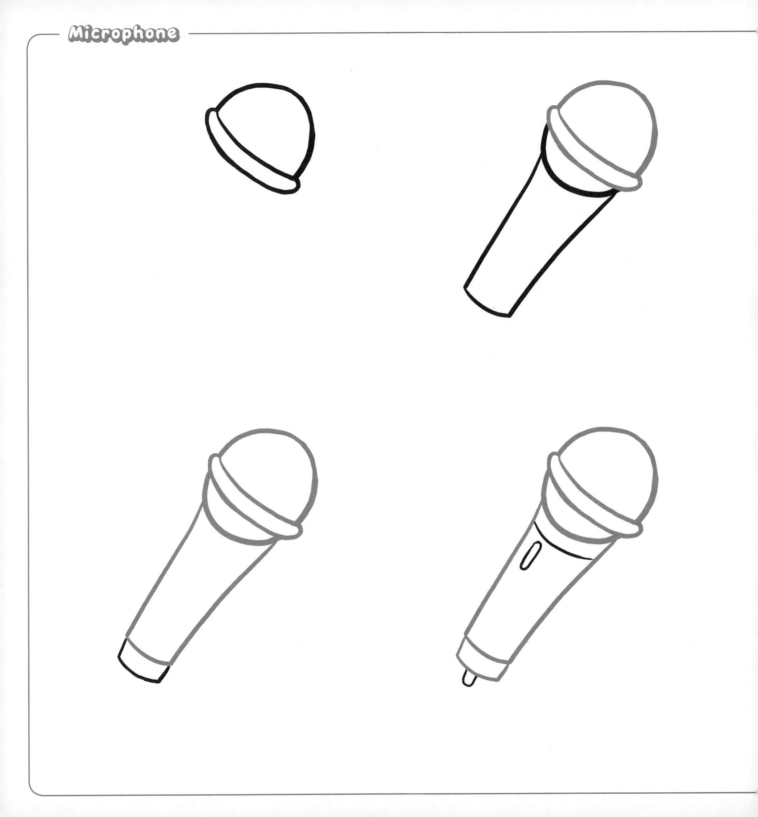

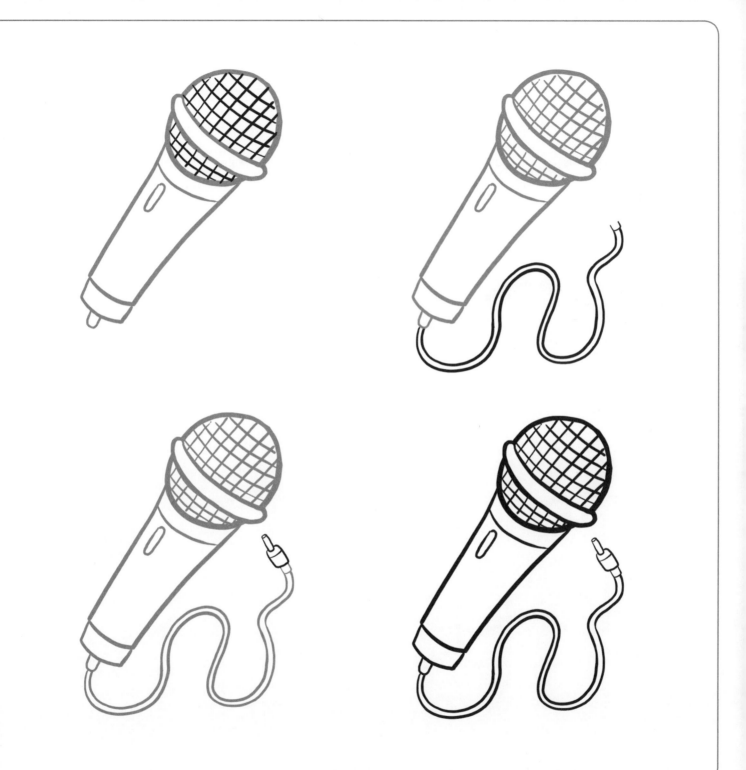

Game controller

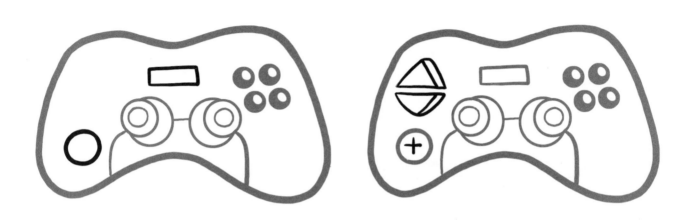

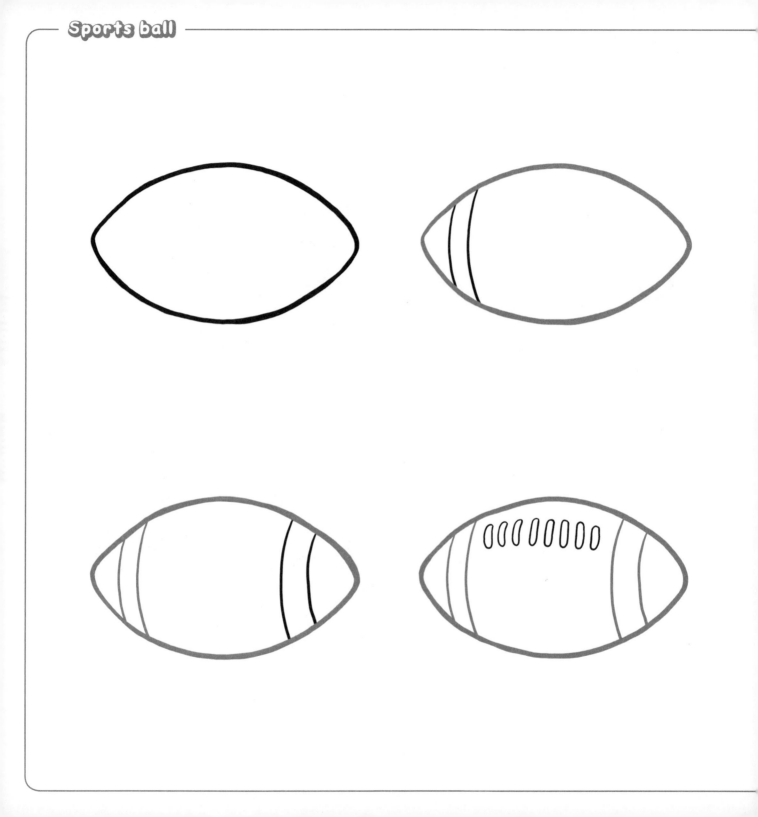

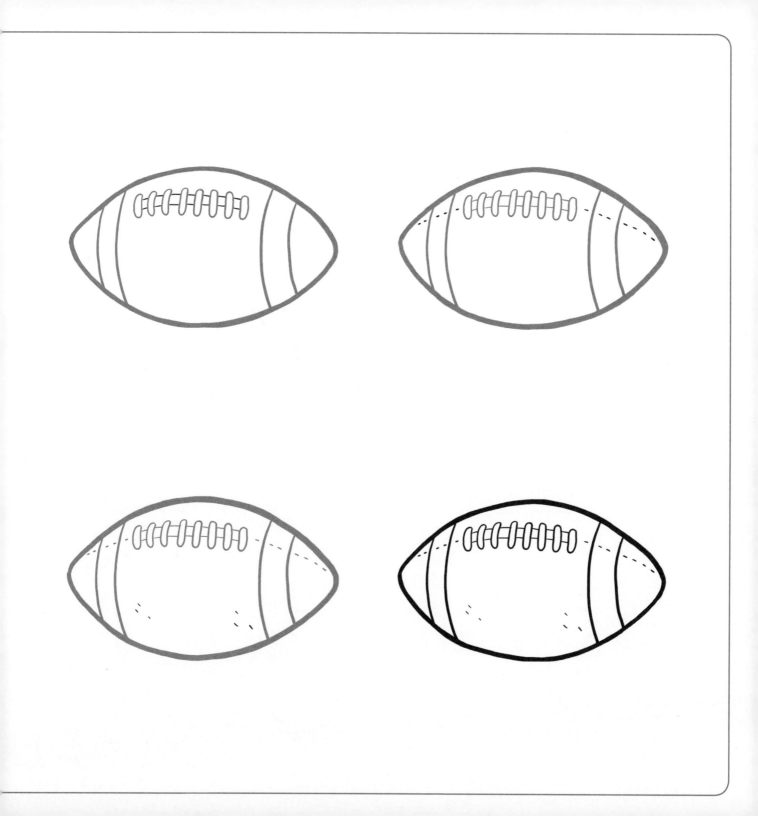

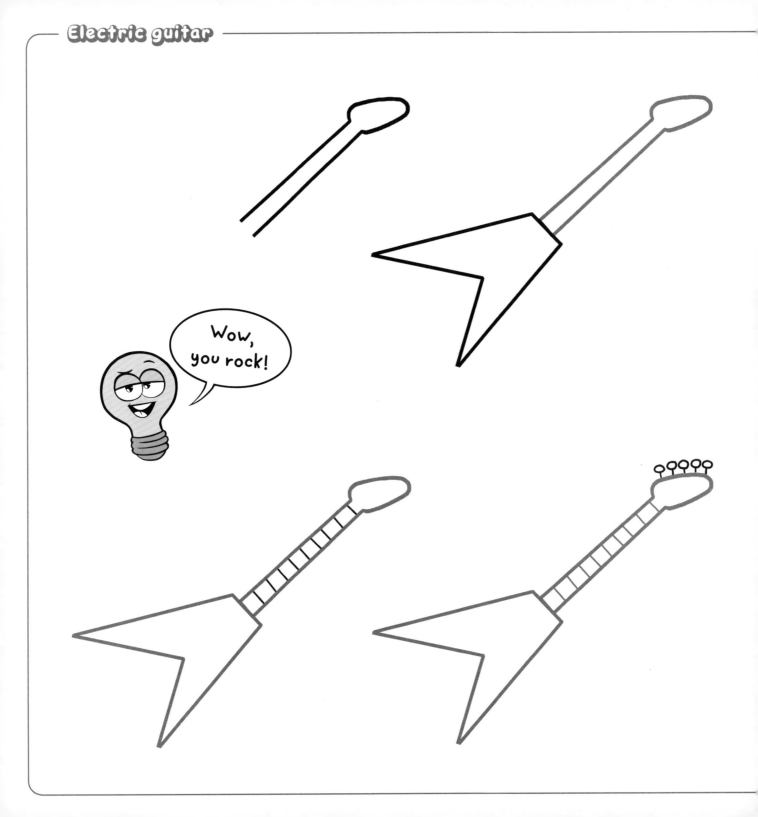

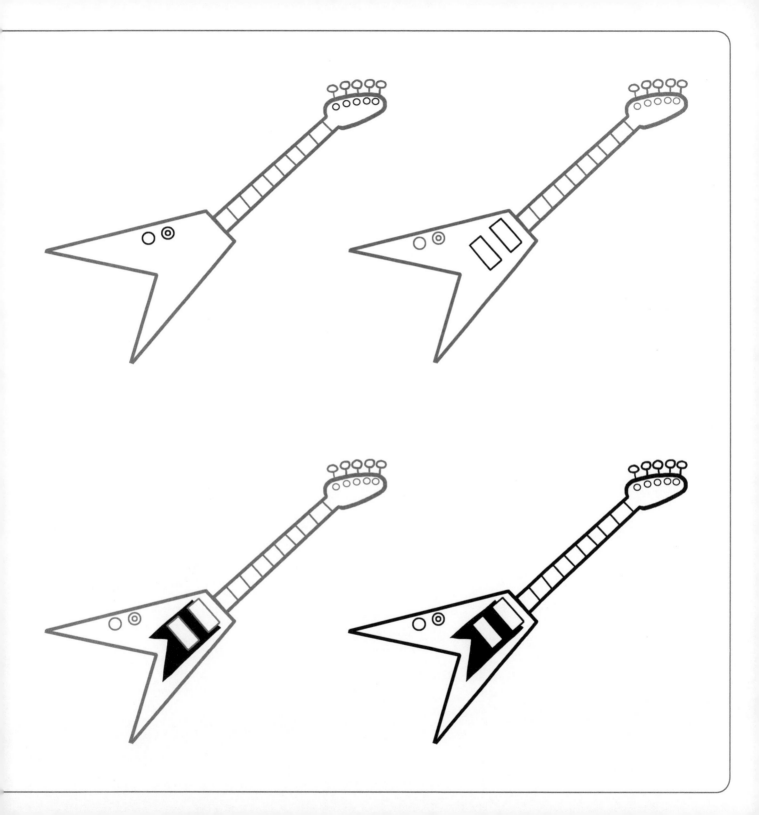

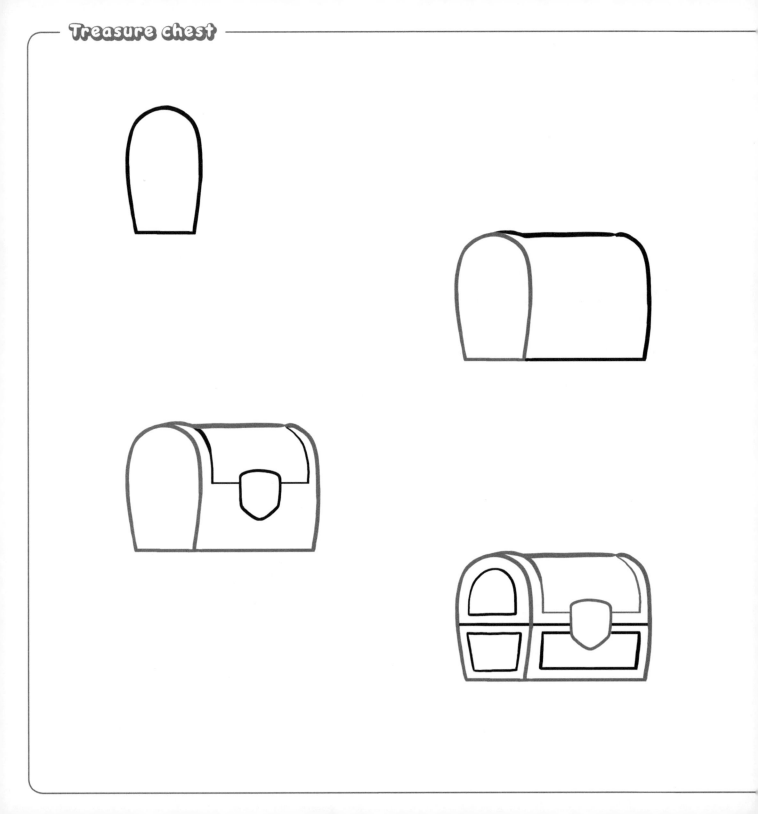

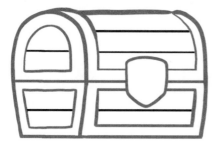

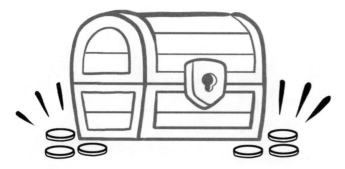

# Try using thinner lines for smaller details.

The stitching and laces have thinner lines **because they are smaller than the rest of the shoe.**

Thin details

Thick outlines

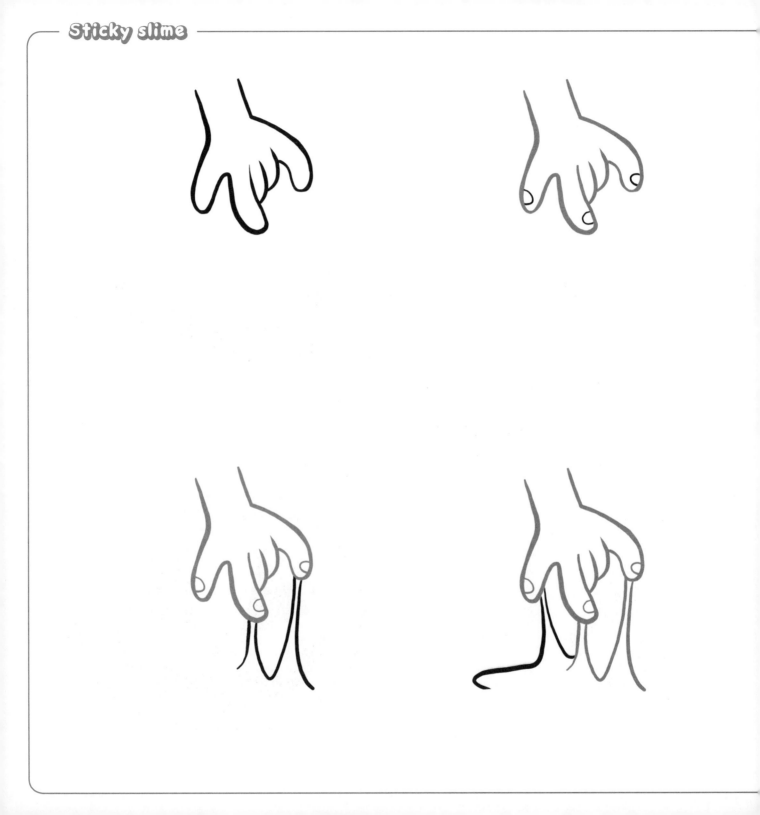

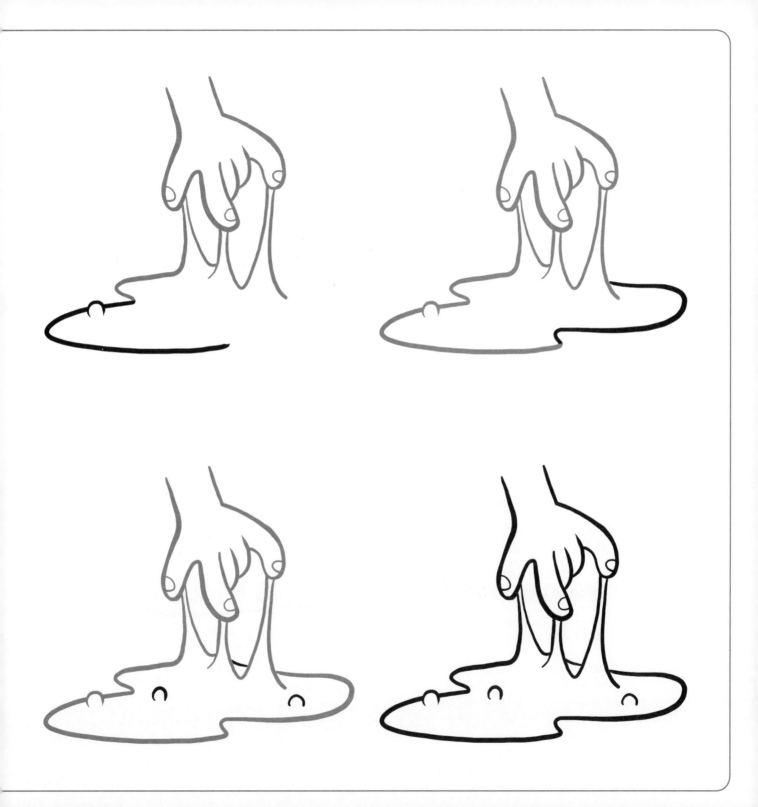

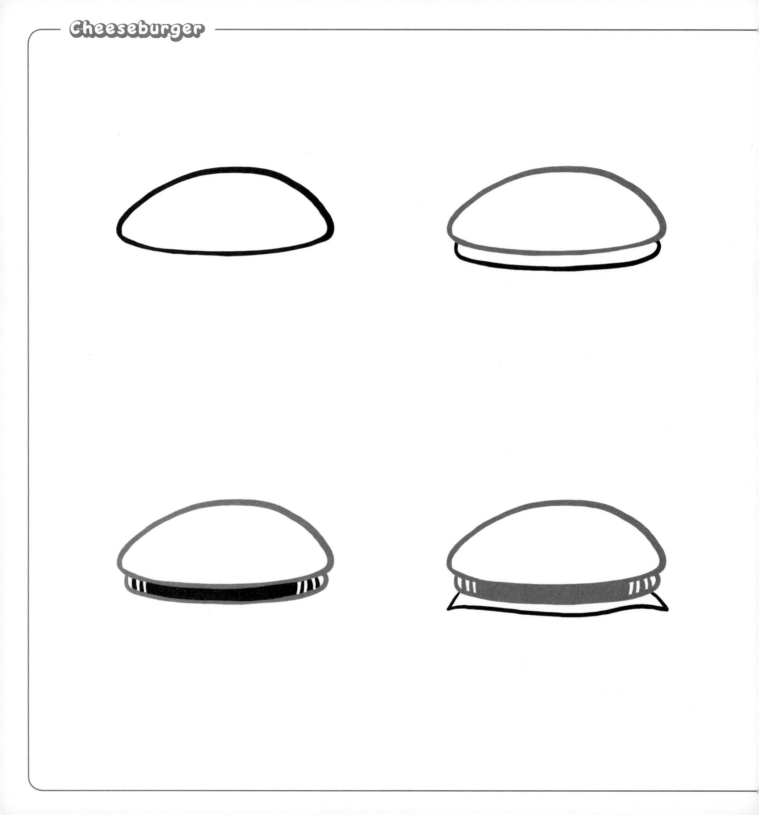

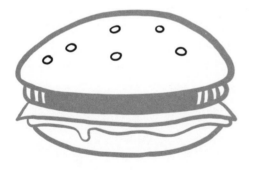

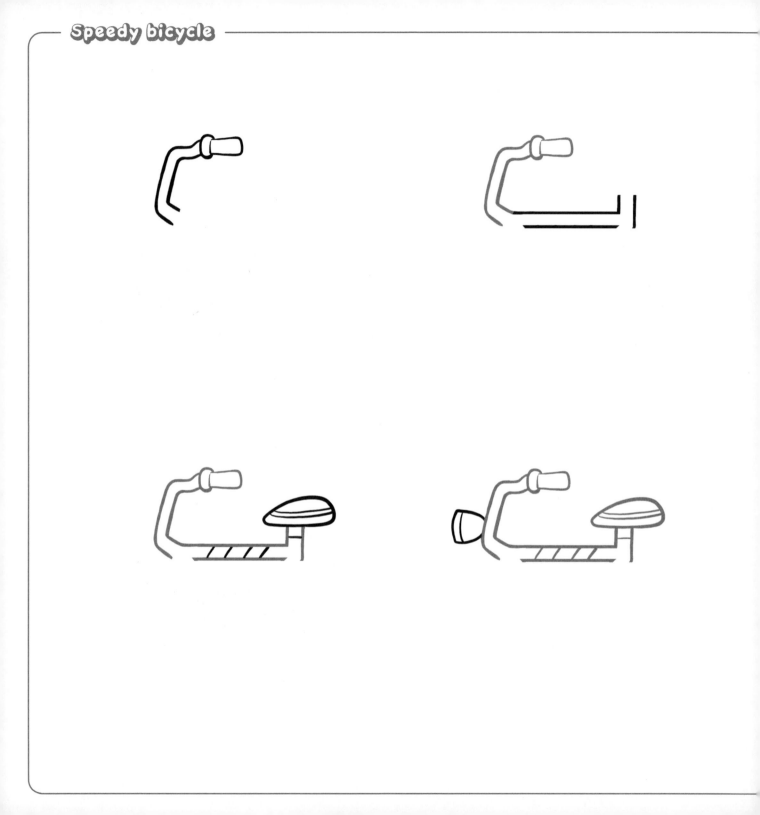

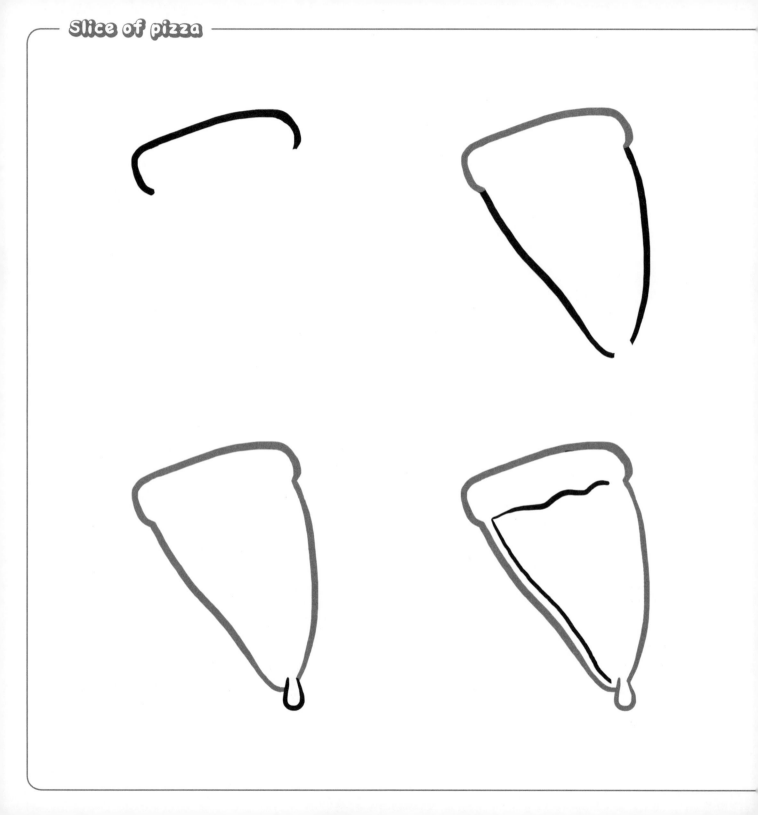

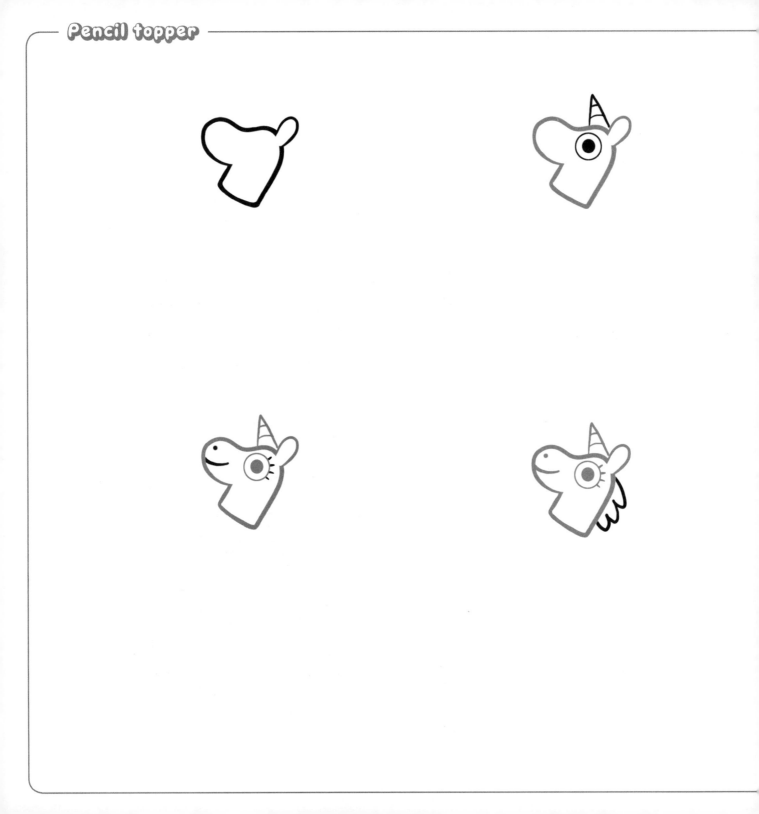

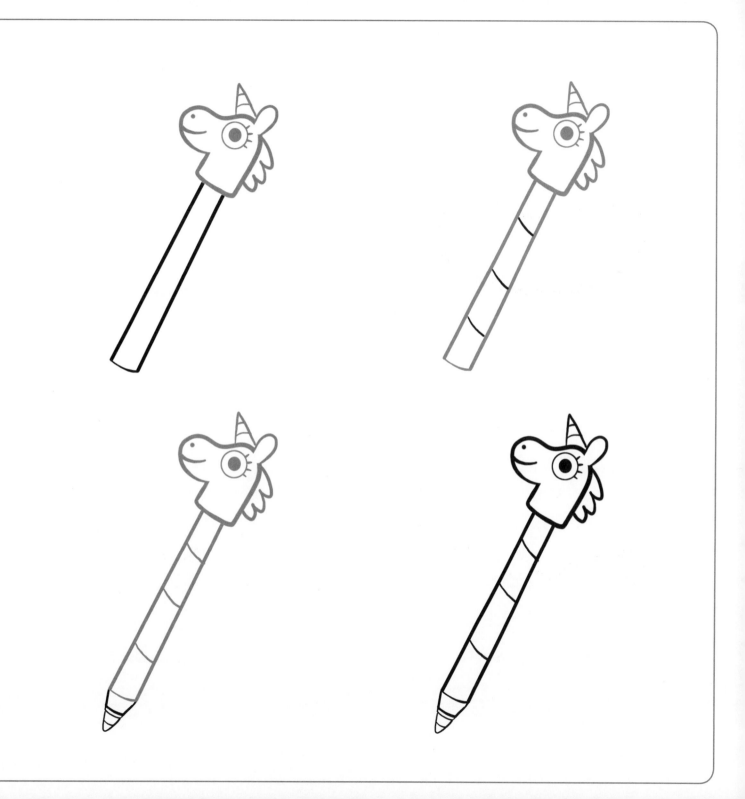

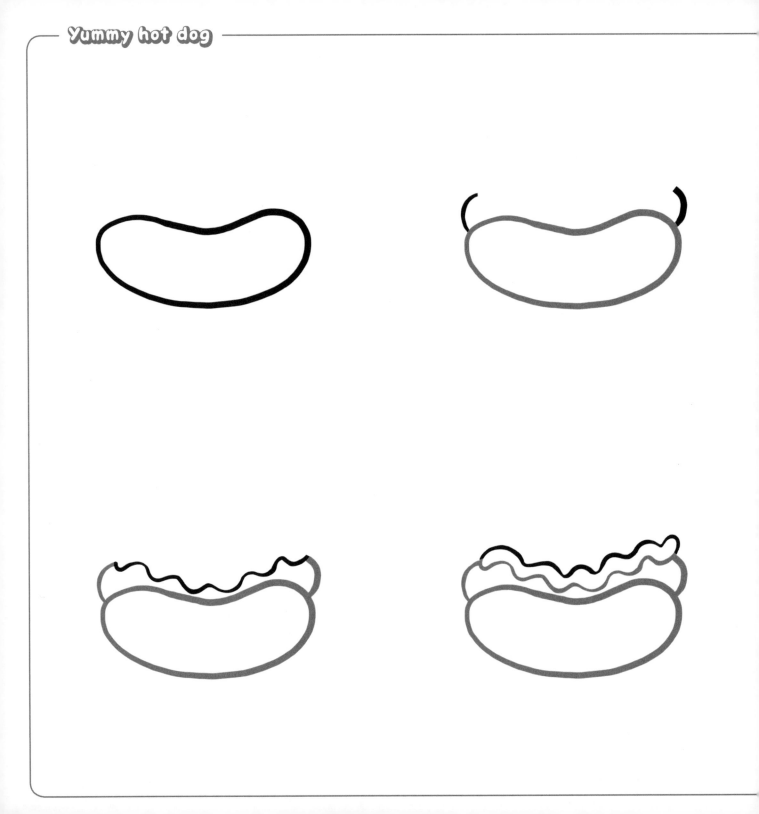

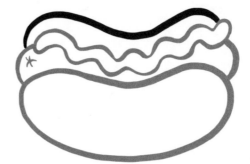

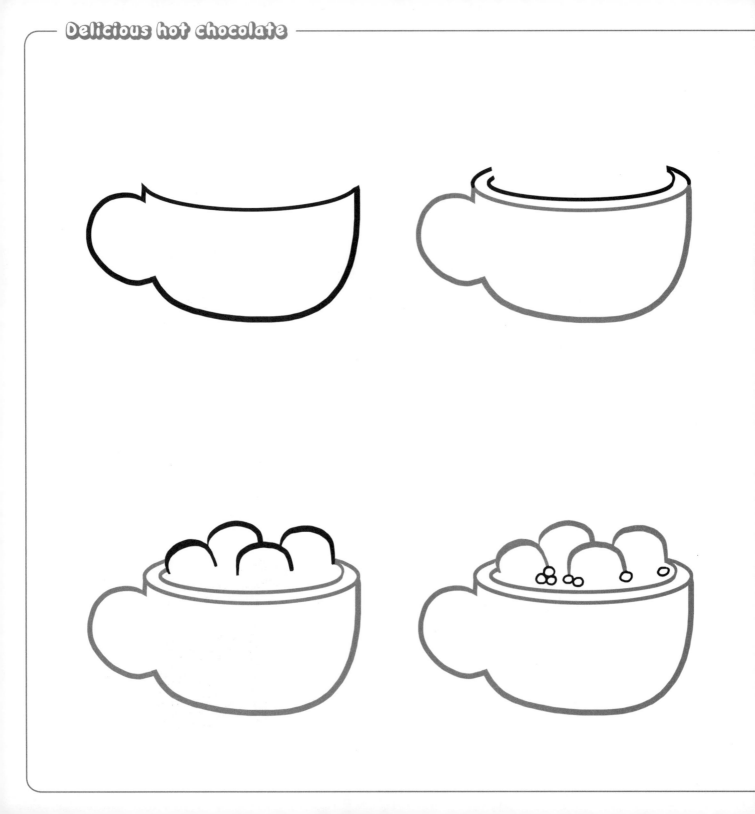

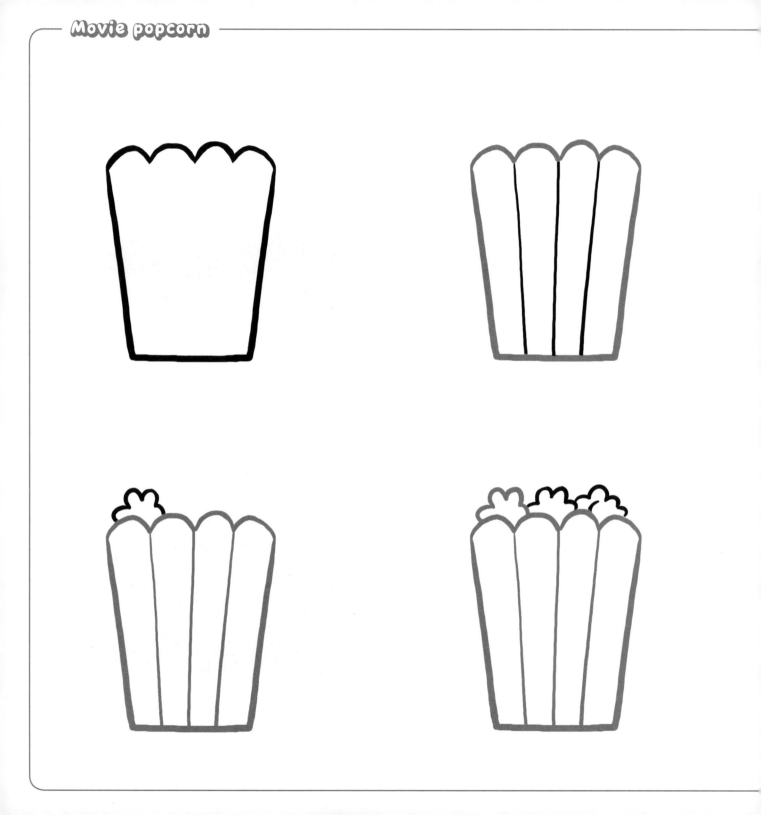

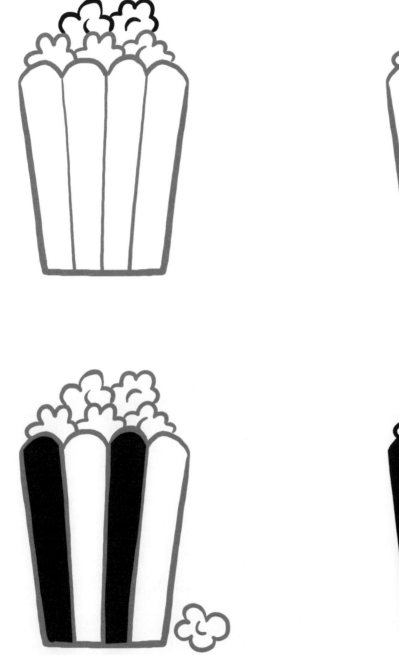

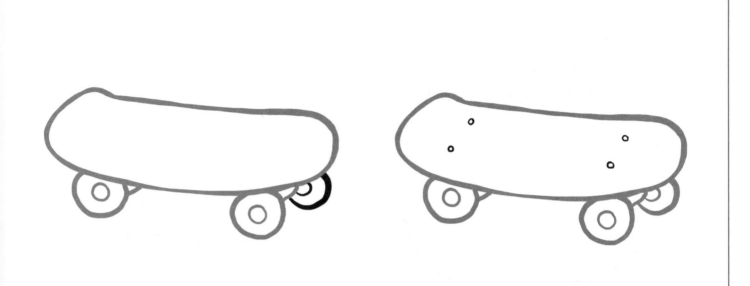

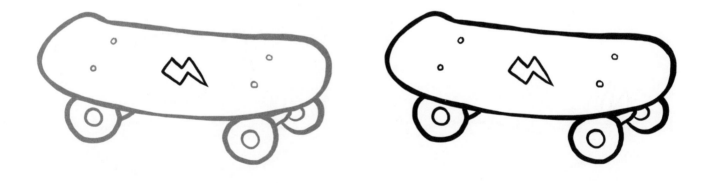

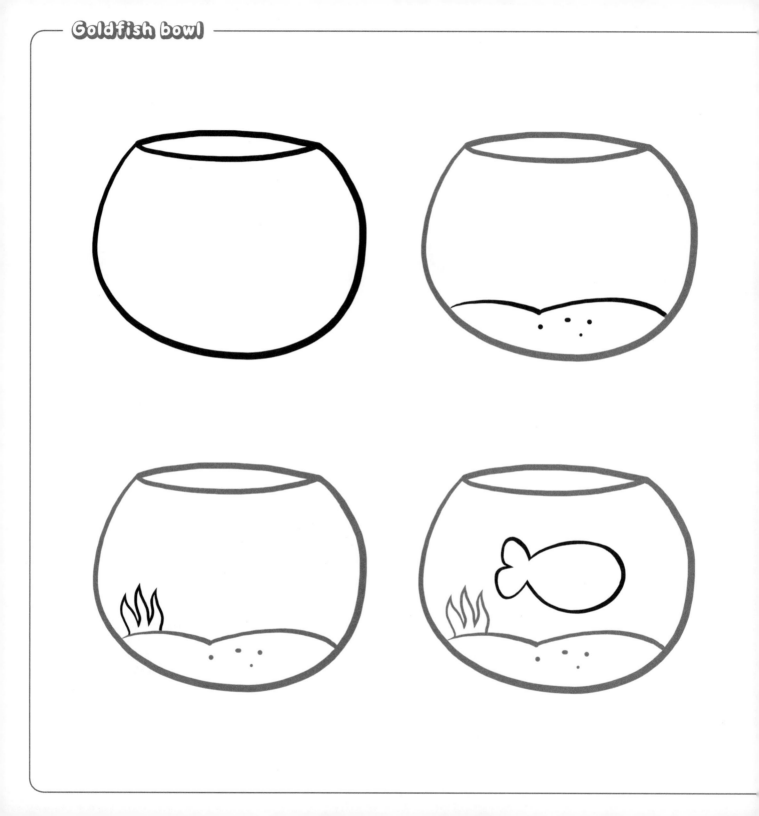

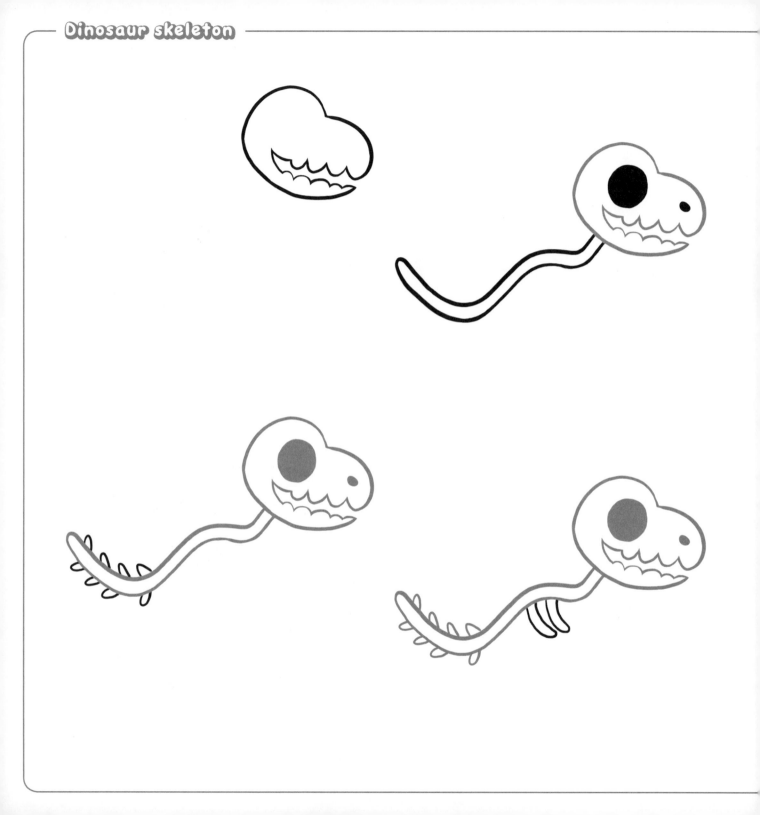

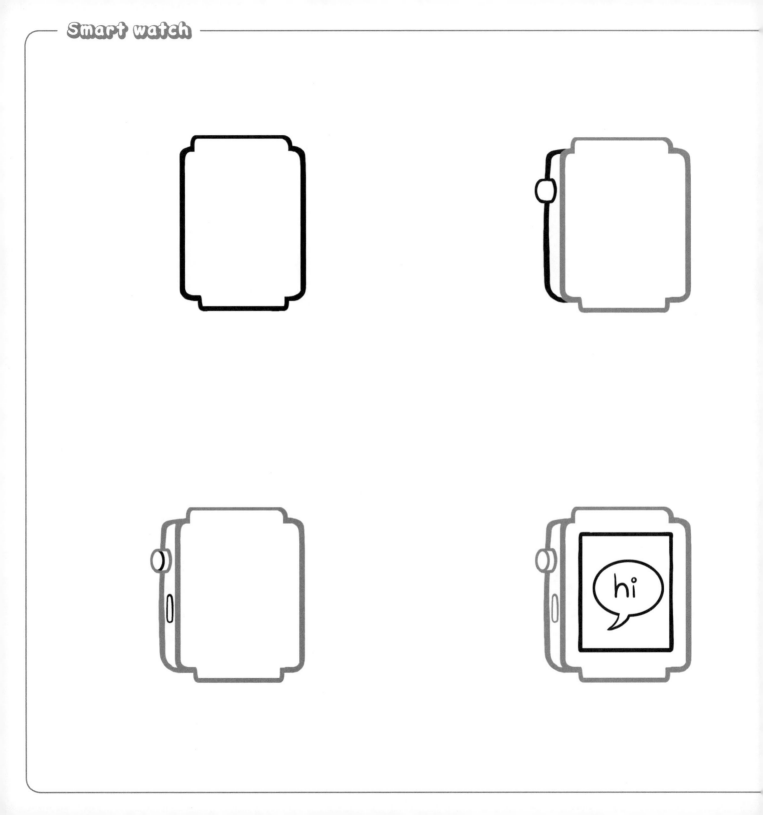

# You've finished this book!

You can go back and practise
drawing the cool things again,
or make up your own.
Have fun drawing!